Ten-Key Skill Builder for Calculators

WILLIAM R. PASEWARK

Pasewark Ltd.
Office Management Consultant
& Professor Emeritus
Texas Tech University

SOUTH-WESTERN
CENGAGE Learning

Australia · Brazil · Japan · Korea · Mexico · Singapore · Spain · United Kingdom · United States

SOUTH-WESTERN
CENGAGE Learning™

Ten-Key Skill Builder for Calculators, Second Edition
William R. Pasewark

VP/Editorial Director: Jack W. Calhoun
Publishing Team Leader: Karen Schmohe
Project Manager: Marilyn Hornsby
Editor: Denise Wheeler
Market Manager: Tim Gleim
Marketing Coordinator: Lisa Barto
Production Coordinator: Jane Congdon
Manufacturing Coordinator: Carol Chase
Art and Design Coordinator: Darren Wright
Development: Thomas N. Lewis
Designer: IMBUE design
Production Services: Lewis Editorial Services
Senior First Print Buyer: Doug Wilke

© 2008 South-Western, a part of Cengage Learning

ALL RIGHTS RESERVED. No part of this work covered by the copyright herein may be reproduced, transmitted, stored, or used in any form or by any means—graphic, electronic, or mechanical, including but not limited to photocopying, recording, scanning, digitizing, taping, Web distribution, information networks, information storage and retrieval systems, or in any other manner—except as may be permitted by the license terms herein.

For product information and technology assistance, contact us at **Cengage Learning Customer & Sales Support, 1-800-354-9706.**

For permission to use material from this text or product, submit all requests online at **www.cengage.com/permissions** Further permissions questions can be emailed to **permissionrequest@cengage.com.**

U.S. Student Edition:
ISBN-13: 978-0-538-69274-8
ISBN-10: 0-538-69274-X

South-Western Cengage Learning
5191 Natorp Boulevard
Mason, OH 45040
USA

Cengage Learning products are represented in Canada by Nelson Education Ltd.

For your course and learning solutions, visit **www.cengage.com**

Acknowledgments
The following schools are gratefully acknowledged for their participation in the study, *Measuring Productivity on the Ten-Key Numeric Keypad Using Strokes a Minute and Errors a Minute*. Many of the findings from this study were used to prepare *Ten-Key Skill Builder for Calculators*.

City	School	Teacher
El Paso, TX	Burges	Ms. O. Zanker
El Paso, TX	Technical Center	Ms. D. Juarez
Euless, TX	Trinity	Ms. D. Innis
Graham, TX	Graham	Ms. J. Buchanan
Greensboro, NC	Ben L. Smith	Ms. G. Nelson
Jacksonville, AR	Jacksonville	Ms. C. Gray
Jacksonville, AR	North Pulaski	Ms. S. Johnson
Little Rock, AR	Mills	Ms. W. Hutchins and Ms. S. Johnson
Little Rock, AR	Oak Grove	Ms. S. Cummings
Little Rock, AR	Robinson	Ms. A. Tenpenny
Lubbock, TX	Coronado	Ms. D. Park
Lubbock, TX	Monterey	Ms. B. Clarkson
Orlando, FL	Oak Ridge	Ms. S. Martin
Pagosa Springs, CO	Pagosa Springs	Mr. D. Bowen
San Antonio, TX	Madison	Ms. B. Kitchens
San Antonio, TX	Roosevelt	Ms. J. Schrader
Seguin, TX	Seguin	Ms. M. Woerndel
Winter Garden, FL	West Orange	Ms. G. Annis

The author thanks Judy Brady, Nell Chapuis, and Diane Hogan, who coordinated the testing program in their cities, and Larry Hess, Heather Pasewark, and Jan Stogner for their contributions.

Printed in the United States of America
10 11 12 13 14 15 13 12 11 10

INTRODUCTION

TO THE TEACHER

The goal of this book is to help students to develop a touch-method mastery of the ten-key numeric keypad in as short a time as possible. The instructional package includes the student text, two forms of the ten-key numeric test, and a Teacher's Edition. The comprehensive Teacher's Edition includes sections on instructional strategy, motivating students, class management, developing effective work habits, grading plans, a sample grading scale, and criteria for determining strokes and errors.

Ten-Key Skill Builder for Calculators is based on a research study measuring productivity on the ten-key numeric keypad using Strokes a Minute and Errors a Minute. Subjects in the study were from 15 high schools in 5 states.

From the findings of this study, the author developed a carefully designed pattern of skill building similar to that used so successfully in keyboarding/typewriting books. These instructional strategies include the following:

1. Technique development using a Technique Checklist; step-by-step introduction to the keypad; illustrations of correct posture, placement of materials at the workstation, and both left- and right-hand finger positions.

2. A scoring system based on Strokes a Minute and Errors a Minute that has been field tested by 416 students.

3. A variety of unique drills to develop mastery: Warm-Up Drills, Speed Drills, Accuracy Drills, Technique Drills, and Review Drills.

4. Drill and Test Records so students have a "running account" of their progress.

5. Motivators that encourage students to achieve self-set goals: SAM and EAM Graphs and a Ten-Key Proficiency Certificate upon completion of the course.

CONTENTS

INTRODUCTION

TO THE STUDENT

Ten-Key Skill Builder for Calculators, in 8 to 12 hours, will give you a mastery of the ten-key numeric keypad. The ten-key numeric keypad is used to input numbers in a wide variety of electronic machines, such as calculators, computers, cash registers, and bank proofing machines.

Ten-Key Numeric Touch Mastery

When you complete this electronic calculator course, you will have learned the ten-key numeric touch method that is used to operate machines in business now and machines that will be used in the future.

Electronic calculators are fast, accurate, and easy to use when operated properly. Therefore, it is important to learn and use only the ten-key touch method from the beginning, rather than looking at the keypad and striking all keys with the same finger. With proper practice, the touch method is faster, more accurate, and uses less head and hand movement in comparison with "hunting and pecking."

Learning Features

This book was based on a study of 416 students learning the touch method. It was written so your learning will be as effective, rapid, and enjoyable as possible. Some of the learning features that will appeal to you include the following:

1. Short, clear instructions with illustrations showing how to master the touch method.

2. A new method of measuring your speed and accuracy using SAM and EAM similar to your typewriting/keyboarding scores.

3. A variety of Warm-Up Drills, Speed Drills, Accuracy Drills, and Technique Drills that will give you a chance to improve each time you work a drill.

4. SAM and EAM Graphs on which you can chart your progress throughout the course.

5. The Ten-Key Proficiency Certificate signed by your teacher that you can present to a prospective employer.

ELECTRONIC CALCULATOR

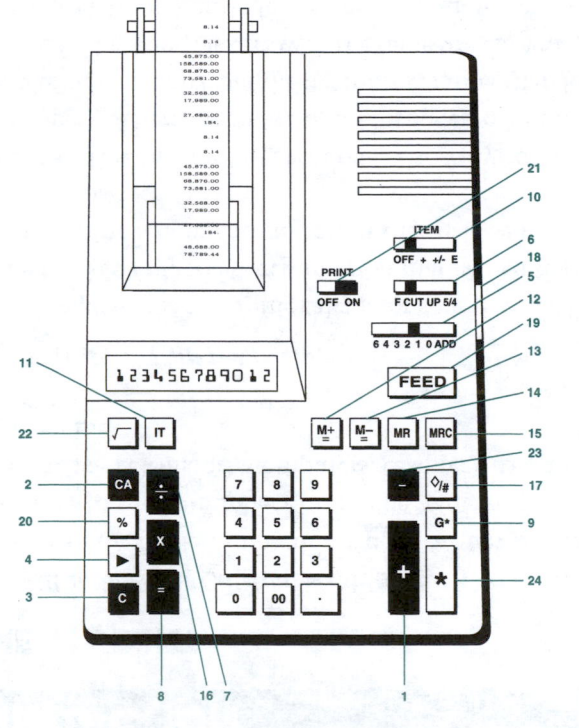

1	Addition Key
2	Clear-All Key
3	Clear Key
4	Clear Right Digit Key
5	Decimal Place Selector
6	Decimal Rounding Selector
7	Division Key
8	Equal Key
9	Grand Total Key
10	Item Count Selector
11	Item Key
12	Memory-Plus (or Memory-Plus/Equals) Key
13	Memory-Minus (or Memory-Minus/Equals) Key
14	Memory-Recall (or Memory-Total) Key
15	Memory-Recall/Clear Key
16	Multiplication Key
17	Non-Add/Sub-Total/Answer-Print Key
18	On/Off Switch
19	Paper Feed Key
20	Percent Key
21	Print Selector
22	Square Root Key
23	Subtraction Key
24	Total Key

ADDITION; TOUCH METHOD: 4, 5, AND 6 KEYS

SKILL GOALS

1. Use the touch method to enter the digits 4, 5, and 6.
2. Solve addition problems.

Getting Ready

1. Clear your desk of everything except your calculator, book, and pencil or pen.
2. Place your book and calculator so you can easily read the book and operate the calculator. You may operate the calculator with either your left hand or right hand.
3. Sit in a comfortable position with your eyes on the copy, fingers on the home keys, back straight, and feet flat on the floor.
4. **Function keys**, such as the Decimal Place Selector [5]*, control the operation of the calculator. You must anticipate the functions needed to solve each group of problems and set the function keys to solve the problems. Set the Decimal Place Selector at *0* and the Item Count Selector [10] at *Off*. If you are using a combination display-printing calculator, set the Print Selector [21] at *On*.

Throughout this workbook, use the bracketed numbers to locate calculator parts on the illustration on page vi.

Position your book and calculator at a comfortable angle.

Left-Hand Operation

Right-Hand Operation

Practice correct posture.

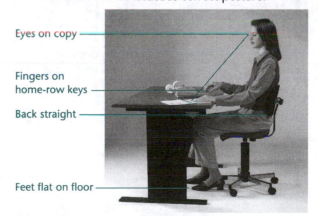

Eyes on copy

Fingers on home-row keys

Back straight

Feet flat on floor

5. Turn your calculator on with the On/Off Switch [18]. A **clear symbol** such as *0*, *0A*, *0C*, or *0.CA* should print on the tape. If it does not, strike the Clear-All Key [2].

Use these *Getting Ready* procedures at the beginning of all future jobs.

Using the Touch Method

The **ten-key numeric touch method** means striking all the numbered keys and some function keys *without looking at the keypad*. The keys are located by "touch" when you keep the index, middle, and ring fingers over the 4, 5, and 6 Keys. These are the **home-row** keys.

It is probably easier to strike keys with your writing hand instead of your opposite hand. However, you may prefer to develop the ten-key numeric touch method using your nonwriting hand, leaving your writing hand free to write answers and turn pages in this workbook.

Keep your hand correctly positioned on the home-row keys—4, 5, and 6.

Left-Hand Operation Right-Hand Operation

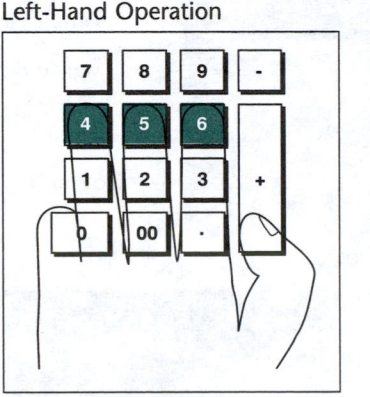
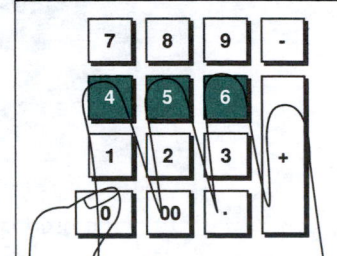

Correct finger placement for the touch method

	Left-Hand Operation (See Illus. above)	Right-Hand Operation (See Illus. above)
Index Finger	6	4
Middle Finger	5	5
Ring Finger	4	6
Little Finger	0	Addition Key, Total Key
Thumb	Addition Key, Total Key	0

Using the Touch Method (continued)

The home-row keys may be more hollow than the other keys, and the 5 Key may have a raised dot to help you find the home row by touch. Keep your wrist straight and your fingers curved over the home-row keys. As you learn to use the home-row keys by touch, emphasize accuracy rather than speed. Use the touch method to complete each step as you read it.

1. LOOK AT THE KEYPAD and use the correct finger to strike the 4 Key three times.

2. Strike the Addition Key [1]. The number *444* has now been printed on the calculator tape.

3. DO NOT LOOK AT THE KEYPAD and strike the 4 Key three times. (If you make a mistake, clear the calculator by striking the Clear-All Key and start the problem again.)

4. Strike lightly the Addition Key. Think of the stroke as a "tap."

5. Strike the Total Key [24] to get your answer (that is, 888). Striking the Total Key will also clear the calculator for the next problem.

6. Repeat Steps 1 through 5 for the 5 Key and then for the 6 Key.

Home-Row Keys

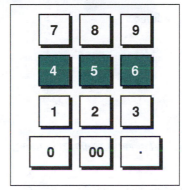

Your tape should look similar to this tape after you have completed Step 6.

0.	CA
444.	+
444.	+
888.	*
555.	+
555.	+
1,110.	*
666.	+
666.	+
1,332.	*

Keep your fingers curved over the home-row keys.

Addition

Always enter **digits** (any figure from 0 to 9) in the same order that you would write them—from left to right. When you are instructed to enter a number or strike a key, *tap* each key with a sharp, quick stroke.

The chart entitled *Procedure for Adding* describes how to work the problem, *4 + 5 + 6*. The first column, "Operation," tells you what to do; the second column shows what is printed on the tape. Each number to be added is called an **addend**. Now, complete the problem, *4 + 5 + 6*, using the touch method.

Touch Method—Problem 1

Remove the Job 1 answer strip from page 53.

Be sure the calculator is clear before starting each problem. Remember that accuracy is your first goal. Concentrate on using the touch method to strike each key with the proper finger as you work Problem 1.

Strike each key sharply and quickly.

When the answer is provided, work each problem until your answer matches the workbook's answer. (See the Sample Tape for Problem 1.)

Procedure for Adding

Operation	Tape*
1. Clear the calculator.	0 • CA
2. Enter the first addend (4).	
3. Strike the Addition Key.	4 • +
4. Enter the next addend (5).	
5. Strike the Addition Key.	5 • +
6. Enter the next addend (6).	
7. Strike the Addition Key.	6 • +
8. Strike the Total Key.	15 • *

Symbols may differ for your calculator.

Touch Method—Problem 1

1.

```
  5
  4
  6
  4
  6
  5
 30
```

0.	CA
5.	+
4.	+
6.	+
4.	+
6.	+
5.	+
30.	*

Sample Tape for Problem 1

Home-Row Keys

Complete Problem 2 by touch. When the answer is not in the workbook, write the answer with pen or pencil in the blank space below the problem. Work the problem a second time.

1. If the second answer is the **same** as the first answer, you can assume that the answer is correct. Write the correct answer on the answer strip.

2. If the second answer is **different** from the first, write it below the first answer and repeat the problem until you get two answers that match. Then write the correct answer on the answer strip.

   Follow these procedures to solve Problems 3 through 15 and for all future jobs.

Completing the Job

After you finish all of the problems in a job, do the following:

1. If you have time, do the job again to improve your rhythm.

2. Submit your work as instructed by your teacher.

3. Turn your calculator off and cover it.

   Follow these instructions to complete all future jobs.

Home-Row Keys

2.	3.	4.	5.	6.	7.	8.
4	66	44	54	55	46	64
5	55	66	56	54	45	45
6	46	55	64	44	64	55
44	45	65	45	66	54	46
55	64	45	66	64	46	66
66	54	46	55	45	56	54
___	___	___	___	___	___	___

9.	10.	11.	12.	13.	14.	15.
66	44	444	555	666	544	654
56	56	555	655	556	454	456
55	54	666	465	554	564	545
54	55	466	566	456	466	454
64	64	556	546	654	544	446
45	46	665	464	464	654	555
___	___	___	___	___	___	___

ADDITION; TOUCH METHOD: 1, 2, 3, 7, 8, 9, 0, AND 00 KEYS

SKILL GOALS

1. Use the touch method to enter the digits 1, 2, 3, 7, 8, 9, 0, and 00.
2. Solve addition problems.

7 and 1 Keys

Remove the Job 2 answer strip from page 53.

1. Place your fingers on the home-row keys: 4, 5, and 6.

2. LOOK AT THE KEYPAD and form a picture in your mind of the reach up to the 7 Key. Practice reaching up to the 7 Key three times **without** actually entering the number.

3. WITHOUT LOOKING AT THE KEYS and keeping your fingers over the home-row keys, work Problems 1 through 5.

Reach up from the 4 Key to strike the 7 Key.

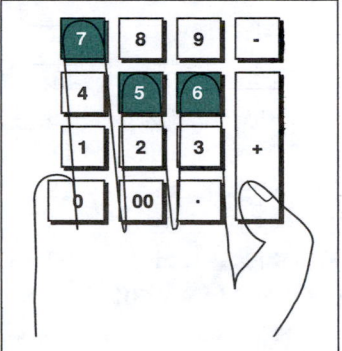

Left-Hand Operation   Right-Hand Operation

7 Key

1.	2.	3.	4.	5.
477	745	7	674	675
777	567	76	756	657
744	746	477	567	667
457	674	756	674	674
755	467	67	747	574

7 and 1 Keys (continued)

4. LOOK AT THE KEYPAD and practice reaching down to the 1 Key three times *without* actually entering the number. Form a picture of this reach in your mind.

5. WITHOUT LOOKING AT THE KEYS, work Problems 6 through 8.

1, 4, and 7 Keys

The 1, 4, and 7 Keys are struck with your ring finger if you use your left hand. If you use your right hand, strike the keys with your index finger. *Without looking at the keypad,* work Problems 9 through 11.

1, 4, 5, 6, and 7 Keys

Work Problems 12 through 17. Repeat these problems until you are comfortable striking the keys at your fastest rate of speed.

Reach down from the 4 Key to strike the 1 Key.

Left-Hand Operation

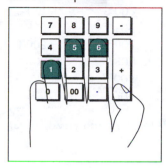

Right-Hand Operation

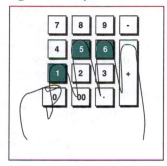

1 Key

	6.	7.	8.
	411	145	1
	111	561	17
	147	146	411
	711	617	156
	145	761	61

1, 4, and 7 Keys

	9.	10.	11.
	771	147	144
	411	417	714
	141	747	441
	717	171	174
	477	114	471

1, 4, 5, 6, and 7 Keys

	12.	13.	14.	15.	16.	17.
	417	165	511	417	111	777
	751	57	674	764	414	715
	14	746	571	145	475	176
	477	641	145	444	147	166
	757	17	617	174	746	147

8, 2, and 00 Keys

The 2, 5, 8, and 00 Keys are struck with the middle finger. Problems 18 through 23 will help you develop stroking patterns so that when you see the numbers *2*, *5*, *8*, and *00*, you will automatically strike these keys with your middle finger. Work Problems 18 through 23 to practice the key reaches.

2, 5, 8, and 00 Keys

Do not look at the keys as you work Problems 24 and 25. Repeat the problems until you are comfortable striking the keys at your fastest rate of speed.

8 Key
Reach up from the 5 Key

18.	19.
588	8
888	85
855	548
568	868
854	84
486	478
648	8
858	48
___	___

2 Key
Reach down from the 5 Key

20.	21.
522	2
222	26
255	682
542	262
24	285
426	528
652	2
252	42
___	___

00 Key
Reach down from the 5 Key

22.	23.
500	200
6,005	5,008
800	800
4,003	5,002
300	500
2,001	8,002
100	200
7,009	8,005
___	___

2, 5, 8, and 00 Keys

24.	25.
2,008	1,258
825	58
528	5,008
800	528
55	84
5,822	85
258	800
8,005	68
___	___

JOB 2

9 and 3 Keys

If you use your left hand, strike the 3, 6, and 9 Keys with your index finger. If you use your right hand, use your ring finger. Work Problems 26 through 29 in the usual manner.

3, 6, and 9 Keys

Do not look at the keys as you work Problems 30 through 33. Repeat the problems until you are comfortable striking the keys at your fastest rate of speed.

9 Key
Reach up from the 6 Key

26.	27.
699	9
999	96
966	916
659	629
954	948
496	89
659	971
949	19

3 Key
Reach down from the 6 Key

28.	29.
633	3
333	37
366	783
653	391
354	133
436	32
653	263
363	35

3, 6, and 9 Keys

30.	31.	32.	33.
969	963	3,693	696
636	693	933	7,613
363	369	63	996
696	639	659	35
939	936	4,563	865
393	396	93	9,345
		6,546	163
		396	7,499

0 Key

If you use your left hand, strike the 0 (Zero) Key with your little finger. If you use your right hand, use your thumb. Work Problems 34 through 37.

All Numeric Keys

Before beginning Job 3, you should be using the touch method to enter all numbers. Problems 38 through 41 will help you use the touch method to locate keys. Repeat the problems until you are comfortable striking the keys at your fastest rate of speed.

0 Key

34.	35.	36.	37.
504	40	630	20
406	10	409	40
601	405	180	204
101	170	250	580
107	60	706	60
706	710	110	930
601	540	103	107
105	70	901	50
____	____	____	____

All Numeric Keys

38.	39.	40.	41.
5,632	9,984	30,340	72,270
60,017	671	3,244	26,100
480	4,926	586	812,433
95	20,010	193	708
3,467	645	793,511	21,883
70,036	2,037	7,759	660
211	89	502	1,131
54	147	17,580	6,172
____	____	____	____

TEN-KEY NUMERIC DRILL

> ### SKILL GOALS
>
> 1. Complete a Ten-Key Numeric Drill (TKNDrill).
> 2. Calculate Strokes a Minute (SAM) and Errors a Minute (EAM).

Technique Checklist

As you complete Job 3, think about how you can improve your techniques to either increase speed or to decrease errors. A Technique Checklist for the Ten-Key Touch Method is on page 40. Following the instructions at the top of the checklist, complete this checklist now to rate your present techniques.

Warm-Up Drill

The Warm-Up Drills at the beginning of each job have been included so that you will practice a variety of number combinations. These drills will help you to move your fingers with rhythm from one key to another using the touch method. The Warm-Up Drill on this page emphasizes the 4, 5, and 6 Keys. Work each problem until each answer matches the workbook's answer.

Warm-Up Drill

4, 5, and 6 Keys

456	564	546	466	565
654	456	625	684	548
545	565	574	294	693
644	564	204	601	705
465	456	598	746	612
656	656	461	352	564
3,420	3,261	3,008	3,143	3,687

Keep your eyes on your book.

JOB 3

Completing Ten-Key Numeric Drill #1

Read all instructions before starting the drill.

Each problem in the Ten-Key Numeric Drill #1 on page 13 has 50 strokes.

A stroke occurs when any numerical key (0 through 9) or function key (such as the Addition Key or Total Key) is entered into the calculator by striking that key. For example, in the number 6,092 there are 5 strokes: 4 strokes for the digits 6092 and 1 stroke for the Addition Key.

Each problem has 50 strokes because you will strike 41 digits, the Addition Key 8 times, and the Total Key once.

Ten-Key Numeric Drill #1, Attempt #1

To complete the drill, do the following:

1. If you have a display-printing calculator, set the

   a. Print Selector at *On*.

   b. Decimal Place Selector at *0*.

2. Complete as many problems as you can in three minutes.

3. If you make an error while working a problem, disregard it and continue entering numbers.

4. Do not compare the answers on the tape to the answers below the problems until you complete the 3-minute timing.

5. Stop immediately at the end of the timing, even if you are in the middle of a number or a problem.

6. Repeat the drill if you finish all 15 problems before the end of three minutes.

Instructions on how to calculate your score begin on page 14.

TEN-KEY NUMERIC DRILL #1

	(A)	(B)	(C)	(D)	(E)
	6,092	734,825	127,434	29,727	411,487
	412,508	6,412	89,451	6,758	34,725
	83,583	87,519	201,985	343,261	2,933
25 strokes →	371,906	195,184	470,197	886,741	886,741
	189,457	65,432	5,762	8,429	56,486
	653,642	879,515	72,581	51,948	82,546
	652	4,098	8,429	16,423	7,442
50 strokes →	82,934	54,267	91,013	757,827	579,818
	3,974	674,523	16,423		
	1,800,774	2,027,128	1,266,847	1,684,570	2,062,178

	(F)	(G)	(H)	(I)	(J)
	236,478	344,513	41,894	4,687	42,132
	518,738	86,374	157,651	962,485	831,228
	7,666	85,622	722,489	31,621	57,582
25 strokes →	15,716	56,712	2,106	357,428	61,846
	731,249	128,469	8,429	96,487	46,252
	189,862	7,854	146,248	15,425	492,873
	44,487	95,223	87,984	184,531	71,742
50 strokes →	625	37,242	15,753	6,452	2,377
		15,753			
	842,009	1,182,554	1,659,116	1,606,032	

	(K)	(L)	(M)	(N)	(O)
	93,172	418,065	15,469	609,305	812,592
	124,609	2,937	269,819	2,275	67,183
	3,312	65,034	4,785	367,011	1,551
25 strokes →	348,705	192,787	794,321	84,496	206,058
	9,155	54,609	135,091	570,322	4,602
	64,088	307,941	2,685	16,682	712,588
	204,913	8,553	44,167	1,934	439,966
50 strokes →	72,506	68,144	80,235	46,099	7,559
	920,460	1,118,070	1,346,572	1,698,124	2,252,099

Calculating Strokes a Minute (SAM) and Errors a Minute (EAM)

After you complete the drill, calculate your scores as follows:

1. Strokes a Minute (SAM)

If you do not finish a problem at the end of the 3-minute timing, count the strokes (numeric digits and function keys) that were completed. For example, in Problem G, if you completed everything through the addend 128,469, the stroke count would be as follows:

Strokes

300	Problems A through F (50 × 6 = 300)
25	Problem G to the 25-strokes marker
7	Problem G for the addend 128,469 and the Addition Key
332	Divided by 3 minutes = 111 Strokes a Minute (SAM)

2. Errors a Minute (EAM)

   a. Compare your answer on the tape with the answer below each problem.

   b. If your answer is different from the answer below the problem, compare each addend and circle each error on the tape.

   c. Add the total number of errors in all problems. For example, if there were three errors in Problem C and one error in Problem E, there would be four total errors.

   d. Divide your total number of errors by 3 minutes to obtain your Errors a Minute (EAM).

Go to the TKNDrill Record on page 36 and record your Total Strokes, Total Errors, SAM, and EAM. Follow the sample line and the instructions on page 37 to complete recording your scores.

Attempt #2

Complete the drill again, following the procedure for Attempt #1. Record your scores on page 36 for Attempt #2.

Attempt #3

Complete the drill again, following the procedure for Attempt #1. Record your scores on page 36 for Attempt #3.

JOB 4

SUBTRACTION; SKILL BUILDER

> ### SKILL GOALS
>
> 1. Use the touch method to solve subtraction problems.
> 2. Increase Strokes a Minute (SAM) or decrease Errors a Minute (EAM) on the Ten-Key Numeric Drill (TKNDrill).

Warm-Up Drill

Review your ratings from Job 3 on the Technique Checklist, page 40. While doing the Warm-Up Drill, strive to improve techniques marked with a zero from Job 3. This Warm-Up Drill emphasizes the 7, 8, and 9 Keys. Do this drill.

Subtraction

Locate the Subtraction Key [23]. If you use your left hand, strike the Subtraction Key with your index finger. For right-hand operation, use your little finger. Keeping your other fingers on the home row, practice reaching to the Subtraction Key three times *without* actually striking the key.

Warm-Up Drill

7, 8, and 9 Keys

789	889	738	475	786
879	799	892	918	269
987	878	809	437	881
897	997	950	803	409
798	898	875	875	582
978	787	409	989	789
5,328	5,248	4,673	4,497	3,716

Strike the Subtraction Key with your index finger.

Left-Hand Operation

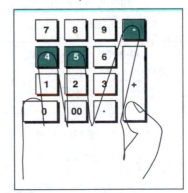

Strike the Subtraction Key with your little finger.

Right-Hand Operation

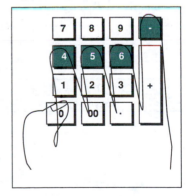

Subtraction (continued)

Remove the Job 4 answer strip and work Problems 1 through 10 by following the *Procedure for Subtracting*.

Subtraction to Correct Errors

The Subtraction Key is used to correct some types of errors. The procedure for correcting errors is explained on pages 41 through 43. Since the purpose of this book is to develop speed and accuracy through drills, do not take time to correct errors except when instructed to do so.

Procedure for Subtracting

Operation	Tape
1. Clear the calculator.	0 • CA
2. Enter the minuend (78).	
3. Strike the Addition Key.	78 • +
4. Enter the subtrahend (53).	
5. Strike the Subtraction Key.	53 • −
6. Strike the Total Key.	25 • *

Subtraction

1.	2.	3.	4.	5.
78	639	643	3,601	1,694
−53	−40	−471	−420	−1,052
25				

6.	7.	8.	9.	10.
890	10,875	2,461	10,397	37,540
−416	−6,361	−932	−650	−8,510
		89	812	934
		−603	−4,056	759
		71	877	−1,265
		426	−4,453	180
		−130	892	−2,002

Skill Builder

How you strike the keys will determine your speed and accuracy. The Technique, Speed, and Accuracy Drills in the Appendix have been carefully designed so you will continuously improve your technique, which will improve your speed and accuracy. Work the following drills:

1. **Technique Drills** A through F, pages 44 and 45.

2. **Speed Drills** A through E, pages 46 and 47. Record your scores on the Speed Drill Record, page 48.

3. **Accuracy Drills** A through E, pages 49 and 50.

Technique Checklist

Complete the Technique Checklist by comparing your techniques from Job 3 with those for this job. Pay special attention to those items marked with a zero in the previous job.

Ten-Key Numeric Drill

1. **Setting Your Goal.** Go to the TKNDrill Record, page 36, and set your TKNDrill goal for Job 4, following the instructions at the bottom of the TKNDrill Record, Item (4).

2. **Meeting Your Goal.** As you complete this drill, think about your goal on the TKNDrill Record. Strive only for speed or only for accuracy. Now, complete TKNDrill #1 on page 13.

3. **Recording Your Scores.** Go to the TKNDrill Record, page 36, and record your scores as you did in Job 3. If you made your goal, circle it on the TKNDrill Record.

Left-Hand Operation

Right-Hand Operation

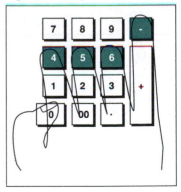

REVIEW; TECHNIQUE, SPEED, AND ACCURACY DRILLS

SKILL GOALS

1. Review addition and subtraction problems using the touch method.
2. Increase SAM or decrease EAM to prepare for Ten-Key Numeric Test #1 (TKNTest #1).

Warm-Up Drill

Review your ratings from Job 4 on the Technique Checklist, page 40. While doing the Warm-Up Drill, strive to improve techniques marked with a zero from Job 4. This Warm-Up Drill emphasizes the 1, 2, and 3 Keys. Work these drill problems in the usual manner.

Skill Builder

To improve your technique, speed, and accuracy, as you did in Job 4, complete the following drills:

1. *Technique Drills* A through F, pages 44 and 45.
2. *Speed Drills* A through E, pages 46 and 47. Record your scores on the Speed Drill Record, page 48.
3. *Accuracy Drills* A through E, pages 49 and 50.

Warm-Up Drill

1, 2, and 3 Keys

123	321	136	241	263
231	213	925	582	932
313	131	871	396	541
312	212	401	571	710
121	323	502	203	358
232	112	603	361	123
1,332	1,312	3,438	2,354	2,927

Practice correct posture.

Technique Checklist

Complete the Technique Checklist by comparing your techniques from Job 4 with those for this job. Pay special attention to those items marked with a zero in the previous job.

Review of Jobs 1 through 4

Remove Job 5 answer strip from page 55 and complete Problems 1 through 15, which review Jobs 1 through 4.

Ten-Key Numeric Drill

Complete TKNDrill #1 on page 13 by following the instructions on page 12.

   If you finish Jobs 1 through 5 in less than five hours, repeat them until you complete five hours of practice. Do this before you take Ten-Key Numeric Test #1 (TKNTest #1) so that your scores can be compared with others who have completed five hours of work.

   Your instructor will administer TKNTest #1.

Addition

1.	2.	3.	4.	5.
30,340	72,270	416	3,771	599
3,244	26,100	61,580	34,886	913
586	812,433	6,088	815	6,782
193	708	38,066	70	26,344
793,511	21,883	169	1,516	262
7,759	660	7,963	21	12,510

Subtraction

6.	7.	8.	9.	10.
8,594	6,001	4,097	3,954	7,050
−6,170	−5,328	−1,553	−2,168	−6,281

11.	12.	13.	14.	15.
739	1,407	858	791	1,441
507	−820	432	517	6,915
−263	240	−616	−1,100	−708
449	−771	−85	65	720
−561	284	808	1,198	−53
273	−175	692	−82	−3,210

Analyzing Progress and Setting Goals

1. Answer Questions 1 and 2 after analyzing your SAM pattern on the Drill Graph—SAM, page 38.

2. Set SAM goals for Jobs 6 through 10 by answering Questions 3 and 4.

3. Answer Questions 5 and 6 after analyzing your EAM pattern on the Drill Graph—EAM, page 39.

4. Set EAM goals for Jobs 6 through 10 by answering Questions 7 and 8.

Strokes a Minute (SAM)

1. Was there a steady increase in SAM on every drill from Job 3 through Job 5?

   Yes _____ No _____ If No, list some reasons why. _____
   _____

2. How many SAM did you increase when comparing the TKNDrill in Job 3 with the TKNDrill in Job 5?

   SAM INCREASE _____

3. How many SAM do you believe you can get by Job 10?

   SAM _____

4. On the TKNTest after Job 10, how many SAM do you believe you can get?

   SAM _____

Errors a Minute (EAM)

5. Were your EAM .33 or less in:

   Job 3   Yes _____ No _____
   Job 4   Yes _____ No _____
   Job 5   Yes _____ No _____

6. In Jobs 3 through 5 if your errors were not .33 or less, list some reasons why. _____
   _____

7. Do you believe you can keep EAM at .33 or less in Jobs 6 through 10?

   Yes _____ No _____

8. On the TKNTest after Job 10, do you believe you can get .33 EAM or less?

   Yes _____ No _____

MULTIPLICATION; SKILL BUILDER

SKILL GOALS

1. Use the touch method to solve multiplication problems.
2. Increase SAM or decrease EAM on the TKNDrill.

Warm-Up Drill

Review your ratings from Job 5 on the Technique Checklist, page 40. While doing the Warm-Up Drill, strive to improve techniques marked with a zero from Job 5. This drill emphasizes the 1, 4, and 7 Keys. Work these drill problems in the usual manner.

Multiplication

Locate the Multiplication Key [16]. If you use your left hand, strike the Multiplication Key with your little finger. For right-handed operation, use your thumb or your index finger. While looking at the keyboard, practice reaching to the Multiplication Key three times *without* actually striking the key.

Remove Job 6 answer strip from page 55 and work Problems 1 through 8 by following the *Procedure for Multiplying*.

Warm-Up Drill

1, 4, and 7 Key

147	478	741	412	159
471	965	417	301	684
717	153	171	567	206
714	204	174	984	317
474	701	747	807	901
141	368	414	519	456
2,664	2,869	2,664	3,590	2,723

Procedure for Multiplying

	Operation	Tape
1.	Enter the multiplicand (4).	•
2.	Strike the Multiplication Key.	4 • ×
3.	Enter the multiplier (5).	
4.	Strike the Equal Key.	5 • =
		20 • *

Multiplication

1.	$4 \times 6 =$	24	5.	$219 \times 651 =$	
2.	$19 \times 4 =$		6.	$9,089 \times 58 =$	
3.	$18 \times 35 =$		7.	$4,977 \times 868 =$	
4.	$526 \times 54 =$		8.	$54,291 \times 312 =$	

JOB 6

Skill Builder

To continue improving your technique, speed, and accuracy, complete the following drills:

1. *Technique Drills* A through F, pages 44 and 45.

2. *Speed Drills* A through E, pages 46 and 47. Record your scores on the Speed Drill Record, page 48.

3. *Accuracy Drills* A through E, pages 49 and 50.

Technique Checklist

Complete the Technique Checklist by comparing your techniques from Job 5 with those for this job. Pay special attention to those items marked with a zero in the previous job.

Ten-Key Numeric Drill

Complete TKNDrill #2 on page 51 as you have done for TKNDrill #1.

Keep your fingers curved over the home-row keys.

DIVISION; SKILL BUILDER

SKILL GOALS

1. Use the touch method to solve division problems.
2. Increase SAM or decrease EAM on the TKNDrill.

Warm-Up Drill

Review your rating from Job 6 on the Technique Checklist, page 40. While doing the Warm-Up Drill, strive to improve techniques marked with a zero from Job 6. This drill emphasizes the 2, 5, and 8 Keys. Complete the drill problems in the usual manner.

Division

Locate the Division Key [7]. If you use your left hand, strike the Division Key with your little finger. For right-hand operation, use your thumb or your index finger. Look at the keyboard. Keeping other fingers on the home keys, practice reaching to the Division Key three times **without** actually striking the key.

Remove the Job 7 answer strip from page 55. Work Problems 1 through 10 by following the **Procedure for Dividing**.

Warm-Up Drill

2, 5, and 8 Keys

152	895	952	258	282
655	562	527	852	828
358	235	482	528	525
652	215	628	582	252
825	548	328	585	228
182	785	152	858	885
2,824	3,240	3,069	3,663	3,000

Procedure for Dividing

	Operation	Tape
1.	Enter the dividend (156).	
2.	Strike the Division Key.	156 • +
3.	Enter the divisor (12).	
4.	Strike the Equal Key.	12 • =
		13 • *

Division

1.	$156 \div 12 =$ ___13___	**6.**	$18,304 \div 88 =$ ___
2.	$375 \div 15 =$ ___	**7.**	$41,275 \div 65 =$ ___
3.	$7,446 \div 73 =$ ___	**8.**	$48,513 \div 471 =$ ___
4.	$1,344 \div 224 =$ ___	**9.**	$309,488 \div 5,336 =$ ___
5.	$7,095 \div 215 =$ ___	**10.**	$65,328 \div 32,644 =$ ___

JOB 7

Skill Builder

To continue improving your technique, speed, and accuracy, complete the following drills:

1. *Technique Drills* A through F, pages 44 and 45.

2. *Speed Drills* A through E, pages 46 and 47. Record your scores on the Speed Drill Record, page 48.

3. *Accuracy Drills* A through E, pages 49 and 50.

Technique Checklist

Complete the Technique Checklist by comparing your techniques from Job 6 with those for this job. Pay special attention to those items marked with a zero in the previous job.

Ten-Key Numeric Drill

Complete TKNDrill #2 on page 51 in the usual manner.

Keep your eyes on your book.

MEMORY; SKILL BUILDER

SKILL GOALS

1. Use the memory register to solve problems.
2. Increase SAM or decrease EAM on the TKNDrill.

Warm-Up Drill

Review your ratings from Job 7 on the Technique Checklist, page 40. While doing the Warm-Up Drill, strive to improve techniques marked with a zero from Job 7. This drill emphasizes the 3, 5, and 7 Keys. Work these drill problems in the usual manner.

Warm-Up Drill

3, 5, and 7 Keys

573	557	534	531	957
735	357	657	754	159
357	335	732	356	751
753	573	354	475	359
375	577	567	157	379
537	733	365	376	173
3,330	3,132	3,209	2,649	2,778

Strive to improve your techniques.
Strike keys with a firm, quick stroke.

Left-Hand Operation

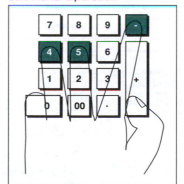

Right-Hand Operation

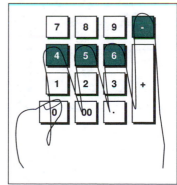

Memory-Plus Key

The Memory-Plus (or Memory-Plus/Equals) Key [12] records a number in the memory register. Work the problem below by following the *Procedure for Memory-Plus Key*.

Example:

1.	3		**2.**	2		**3.**	Grand
	+8	+		+6	=		Total
	11			8			19

Procedure for Memory-Plus Key

Operation	Tape[1]
1. To clear the operating register and memory register, strike the Clear-All Key.[2]	0 *
2. Enter the first addend (3) and strike the Addition Key.	3 ● +
3. Enter the second addend (8) and strike the Addition Key.	8 ● +
4. Strike the Total Key.	11 ● *
5. Strike the Memory-Plus Key.	11 M +
6. Enter the first addend (2) and strike the Addition Key.	2 ● +
7. Enter the second addend (6) and strike the Addition Key.	6 ● +
8. Strike the Total Key.	8 ● *
9. Strike the Memory-Plus Key.	8 M +
10. Strike the Memory-Recall (or Memory-Total) Key [14].	19 ● M *

[1]*On some calculators, the symbols may appear different from those in this illustration.*

[2]*On some calculators, it may be necessary to strike another key.*

JOB 8

Memory-Plus Key (continued)

Remove the Job 8 answer strip from page 57 and complete the problems by following these instructions.

To work Problems 1 through 8, do the following:

1. Clear the operating register and memory register by striking the Clear-All Key. On some calculators, it may be necessary to strike another key.

2. Work Problem 1 and compare your sum with the sum below the problem.

3. Add the sum to the memory register by striking the Memory-Plus Key.

4. Clear the operating register before adding the next group of addends (in Problem 2) by striking the Total Key or Clear Key [3]. Do not clear the memory until you have calculated the Grand Total.

5. Repeat Steps 2 through 4 for each group of numbers and record your answer below the problem.

6. To obtain the Grand Total, strike the Memory-Recall Key.

Memory-Plus Key

1.		2.		3.		4.
7,534		552		8,153		
1,564		8,976		661		Grand
8,741		523		471		Total
4,689		715		894		
_____	+	_____	+	_____	=	_____

5.		6.		7.		8.
2,504		317		6,043		
7,366		5,049		576		Grand
1,452		976		340		Total
3,310		842		889		
_____	+	_____	+	_____	=	_____

JOB 8   Memory; Skill Builder

JOB 8

Memory-Minus Key

The Memory-Minus (or Memory-Minus/Equals) Key [13] subtracts a number from the memory register. To work Problems 9 through 12, follow the instructions for the Memory-Plus Key, but this time strike the Memory-Minus Key after working Problem 10 and after working Problem 11.

Memory-Plus and Memory-Minus Keys

To work Problems 13 through 16, follow the instructions for the Memory-Plus Key, but add the first column, subtract the second column, and add the third column.

Memory-Minus Key

9.	10.	11.	12.
74,827	164	8,579	
5,677	8,500	2,374	Grand
1,598	7,557	5,746	Total
3,435	4,246	8,933	
_____ −	_____ −	_____ =	_____

Memory-Plus and Memory-Minus Keys

13.	14.	15.	16.
879	101	931	
475	874	53	Grand
725	854	571	Total
812	52	64	
974	883	461	
_____ −	_____ +	_____ =	_____

Multiplication and Memory

To work Problems 17 through 26, do the following:

1. Clear the operating register and the memory register.

2. Enter the multiplicand and strike the Multiplication Key.

3. Enter the multiplier. To enter the product into the memory, determine if your calculator has a MemoryPlus/Equals Key [12]:

   a. If it does, strike this key and the product will be added to the memory.

   b. If it does not, strike the Equal Key, then the Memory-Plus Key.

4. Record the product.

5. Unlike addition and subtraction using memory, it is not necessary to clear the operating register before entering the next problem. When you strike the first key for the next multiplicand, the product automatically clears from the operating register.

6. Repeat Steps 2 through 5 for each set of factors.

7. Strike the Memory-Recall Key to obtain the Grand Total.

Division and Memory

To work Problems 27 through 36, follow the instructions for multiplication but enter the dividend and strike the Division Key in Step 2. Then enter the divisor and continue as described in Steps 3 through 7.

Multiplication and Memory

17. $25 \times 8 =$ _____

18. $11 \times 9 =$ _____

19. $12 \times 4 =$ _____

20. $14 \times 6 =$ _____

21. Grand Total = _____

22. $8,812 \times 5 =$ _____

23. $18 \times 7,890 =$ _____

24. $10 \times 12,699 =$ _____

25. $710 \times 94 =$ _____

26. Grand Total = _____

Division and Memory

27. $60 \div 3 =$ _____

28. $975 \div 25 =$ _____

29. $980 \div 10 =$ _____

30. $552 \div 23 =$ _____

31. Grand Total = _____

32. $6,776 \div 11 =$ _____

33. $98,672 \div 56 =$ _____

34. $32,480 \div 140 =$ _____

35. $25,916 \div 62 =$ _____

36. Grand Total = _____

Keep your fingers curved over the home-row keys.

Skill Builder

To continue improving your technique, speed, and accuracy, complete the following drills.

1. *Technique Drills* A through F, pages 44 and 45.

2. *Speed Drills* A through E, pages 46 and 47. Record your scores on the Speed Drill Record, page 48.

3. *Accuracy Drills* A through E, pages 49 and 50.

Technique Checklist

Complete the Technique Checklist by comparing your techniques from Job 7 with those for this job. Pay special attention to those items marked with a zero in the previous job.

Ten-Key Numeric Drill

Complete TKNDrill #2, page 51 in the usual manner.

JOB 9

IMPROVING SPEED AND ACCURACY

> **SKILL GOALS**
>
> 1. Improve speed and accuracy by practicing drills.
> 2. Increase SAM or decrease EAM on the TKNDrill.

Warm-Up Drill

Review your ratings from Job 8 on the Technique Checklist, page 40. While doing the Warm-Up Drill, strive to improve techniques marked with a zero from Job 8. This drill emphasizes the 1, 5, and 9 Keys. Work these drill problems in the usual manner.

Stroking Sequence Patterns

Improving your control over the sequence in which keys are struck will help you increase SAM and decrease EAM. Stroking Sequence Problems in this job have a variety of patterns, as shown in the Stroking Sequence Patterns diagrams.

Warm-Up Drill
1, 5, and 9 Keys

195	191	995	959	591
199	955	115	119	999
519	515	551	959	911
159	951	911	559	515
151	599	551	511	195
915	591	991	155	599
2,138	3,802	4,114	3,262	3,810

Stroking Sequence Patterns

(4, 8, 6)   (1, 5, 3)  (7, 5, 9)

(4, 2, 6)  (1, 5, 7)  (3, 5, 9)

Stroking Sequence Problems

Remove the Job 9 answer strip and complete Problems 1 through 12. The purpose of these problems is to help you increase speed and accuracy. Strive to increase your SAM and decrease your EAM as you complete each problem.

Skill Builder

To continue improving your technique, speed, and accuracy, complete these drills:

1. *Technique Drills* A through F, pages 44 and 45.

2. *Speed Drills* A through E, pages 46 and 47. Record your scores on the Speed Drill Record, page 48.

3. *Accuracy Drills* A through E, pages 49 and 50.

Technique Checklist

Complete the Technique Checklist by comparing your techniques from Job 8 with those for this job. Pay special attention to those items marked with a zero in the previous job.

Ten-Key Numeric Drill

Complete TKNDrill #2 in the usual manner.

Stroking Sequence Problems

4, 8, and 6 Keys		1, 5, and 3 Keys		7, 5, and 9 Keys	
1.	**2.**	**3.**	**4.**	**5.**	**6.**
466	886	313	513	975	759
464	448	153	531	755	975
646	668	351	315	799	555
888	644	533	135	995	777
846	884	511	351	559	999
___	___	___	___	___	___

4, 2, and 6 Keys		1, 5, and 7 Keys		3, 5, and 9 Keys	
7.	**8.**	**9.**	**10.**	**11.**	**12.**
624	246	751	551	935	359
244	624	571	771	355	935
266	444	517	117	399	555
664	222	115	555	995	333
426	666	775	777	559	999
___	___	___	___	___	___

REVIEW; TECHNIQUE, SPEED, AND ACCURACY DRILLS

SKILL GOALS

1. Review multiplication, division, and memory problems using the touch method.
2. Increase SAM or decrease EAM to prepare for Ten-Key Numeric Test #2 (TKNTest #2).

Warm-Up Drill

Review your ratings from Job 9 on the Technique Checklist, page 40. While doing the Warm-Up Drill, strive to improve techniques marked with a zero from Job 9. This drill emphasizes the 3, 5, and 9 Keys. Work these problems in the usual manner.

Review of Jobs 6 through 9

These problems review Jobs 6 through 9. Remove the Job 10 answer strip and complete Multiplication, Division, and Memory Problems 1 through 27 on this page and page 34.

Warm-Up Drill

3, 5, and 9 Keys

953	999	993	956	321
359	555	553	354	456
539	333	559	583	989
593	335	593	529	852
935	339	539	153	369
395	995	953	959	941
3,774	3,556	4,190	3,534	3,928

Multiplication

1.	$12 \times 9 =$	_____
2.	$59 \times 48 =$	_____
3.	$968 \times 66 =$	_____
4.	$759 \times 244 =$	_____
5.	$1,329 \times 244 =$	_____

Division

6.	$18 \div 2 =$	___
7.	$47 \div 47 =$	___
8.	$999 \div 37 =$	___
9.	$724 \div 181 =$	___
10.	$8,326 \div 181 =$	___

Skill Builder

To continue improving your technique, speed, and accuracy, complete these drills:

1. **Technique Drills** A through F, pages 44 and 45.

2. **Speed Drills** A through E, pages 46 and 47. Record your scores on the Speed Drill Record, page 48.

3. **Accuracy Drills** A through E, pages 49 and 50.

Technique Checklist

Complete the Technique Checklist by comparing your techniques from Job 9 with those for this job. Pay special attention to those items marked with a zero in the previous job.

Ten-Key Numeric Drill

To prepare for TKNTest #2 that will be administered by your instructor, work TKNDrill #2, page 51.

If you completed Jobs 1 through 10 in less than 10 hours of practice, repeat them until you complete 10 hours of practice. Do this before you take TKNTest #2 so that your scores can be compared with others who have completed 10 hours of work.

If you have time before taking TKNTest #2, repeat the Skill Builder.

Addition Using Memory

11.	12.	13.	14.
1,492	1,801	225	
687	394	168	Grand
412	2,202	1,003	Total
2,280	413	986	
——— +	——— +	——— =	———

Subtraction Using Memory

15.	16.	17.	18.	19.
548	47	24	472	
53	42	473	263	
364	223	30	312	Grand
2,220	10	120	1,235	Total
206	343	37	435	
——— −	——— +	——— −	——— =	———

Multiplication Using Memory

20. $8,786 \times 2,149 =$ _____

21. $568 \times 102 =$ _____

22. $37,282 \times 405 =$ _____

23. Grand Total = _____

Division Using Memory

24. $648 \div 12 =$ _____

25. $6,345 \div 45 =$ _____

26. $860 \div 20 =$ _____

27. Grand Total = _____

Analyzing Progress

1. Answer Questions 1 and 2 after analyzing your SAM pattern on the Drill Graph—SAM, page 38.

2. Answer Question 3 about SAM.

3. Answer Questions 4 and 5 after analyzing your EAM pattern on the Drill Graph—EAM, page 39.

4. Answer Question 6 about EAM.

Strokes a Minute (SAM)

1. Was there a steady increase in SAM on every drill from Job 6 through Job 10? Yes _____ No _____

   If No, list some reasons why. _____

   _____

2. How many SAM did you increase when comparing the TKNDrill in Job 6 with the last TKNDrill in Job 10?

   SAM INCREASE _____

3. Did you reach your SAM goal for Job 10 that you set in Job 5? Yes _____ No _____ If No, list some reasons why.

   _____

   _____

Errors a Minute (EAM)

4. Were your EAM less than .33 for:

   Job 6   Yes _____ No _____   Job 9   Yes _____ No _____

   Job 7   Yes _____ No _____   Job 10   Yes _____ No _____

   Job 8   Yes _____ No _____

5. In Jobs 6 through 10 if your errors were not .33 or less, list some reasons why. _____

   _____

6. Did you reach your EAM goal for Job 10 that you set in Job 5? Yes _____ No _____ If No, list some reasons why.

   _____

   _____

Improving Your Skill

To continue improving your technique, speed, and accuracy, work through this book again. Obtain the Test Record—Repeat Jobs form from your instructor so you can record your scores for 15, 20, 25, and 30 hours. To record these scores on the Drill Graph—SAM and Drill Graph—EAM, pages 38 and 39, use a different color pencil or pen for 15, 20, 25, and 30 hours than for your previous scores.

TEN-KEY NUMERIC DRILL RECORD (TKNDRILL RECORD)

Name _____

Job	Date	Attempt	Total Strokes	(1) Actual SAM	Total Errors	(2) Actual EAM	(3) Best of 3 Attempts		(4) Goal		Comments
							SAM	EAM	SAM	EAM	
Sample	9/6	1 2 3	230 275 267	77 92 89	2 3 1	.67 1.00 .33	89	.33	85	.33	*Keep eyes on copy to decrease EAM.*
3		1 2 3							No Goals for Job 3		
4		1 2 3									
5		1 2 3									
6		1 2 3									

Job	Date	Attempt	Total Strokes	(1) Actual SAM	Total Errors	(2) Actual EAM	(3) Best of 3 Attempts SAM	EAM	(4) Goal SAM	EAM	Comments
7		1 2 3									
8		1 2 3									
9		1 2 3									
10		1 2 3									

(1) Divide Total Strokes by 3 to get Actual SAM.

(2) Divide Total Errors by 3 to get Actual EAM.

(3) Record the best of three attempts here and in the blank spaces on the Drill Graph—SAM and the Drill Graph—EAM (Appendixes B and C).

(4) Set your goals, starting with Job 4, *before* beginning the TKNDrill by following these instructions. On the previous TKNDrill, if you made

    a. .33 EAM or fewer, increase your SAM goal 10 strokes higher than the score for your Best Attempt on the previous TKNDrill and set EAM at .33.

    b. more than .33 EAM, set your EAM goal at .33 errors and set SAM the same as on the previous TKNDrill.

DRILL GRAPH—SAM

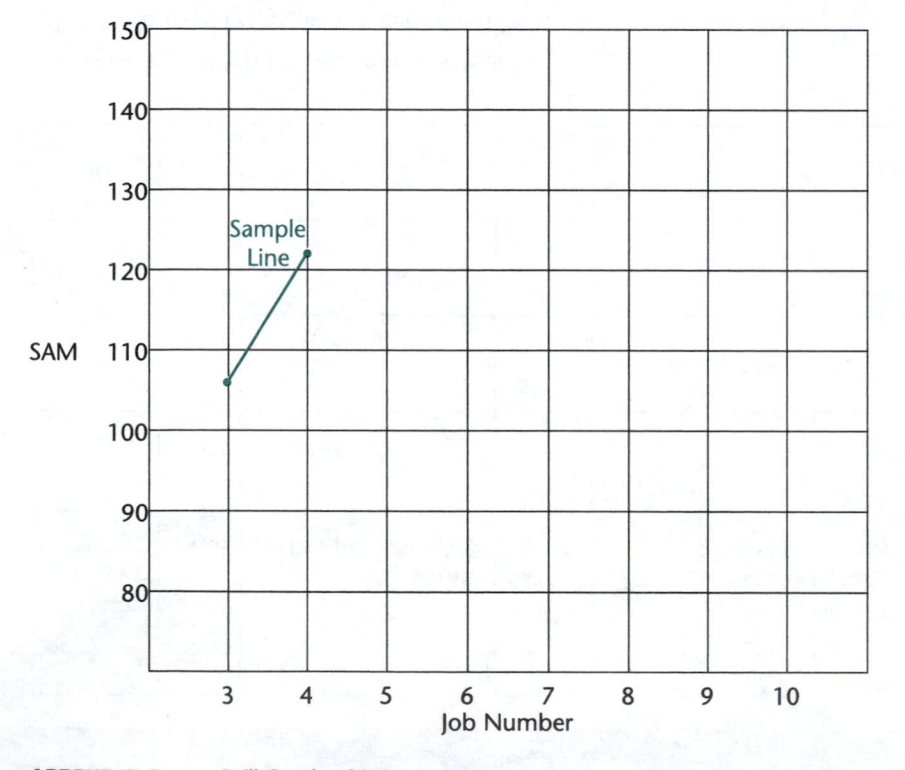

The purpose of this graph is to chart your Strokes a Minute progress from Job 3 through Job 10. Get your SAM from the **Best of 3 Attempts** column on the TKNDrill Record, page 36.

For Job 3, place a dot where the vertical and horizontal lines intersect for the Job Number and SAM. (For the sample line it is at Job 3, 106 SAM.)

For Job 4 through Job 10, follow the procedure for Job 3 above. (For the sample line the intersection is at Job 4, 123 SAM.) Connect the dots with a line from the previous job to the present job. Increases in Strokes a Minute will be shown by an upward sloping line.

DRILL GRAPH—EAM

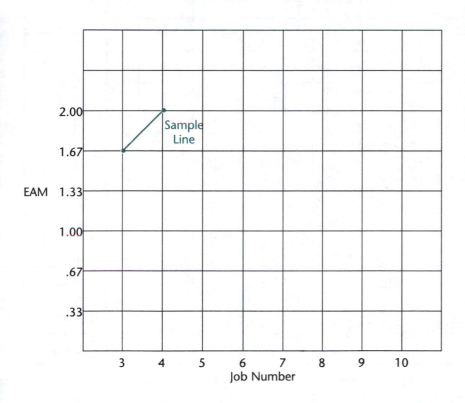

EAM

Sample Line

Job Number

The purpose of this graph is to chart your Errors a Minute progress from Job 3 through Job 10. Get your EAM from the **Best of 3 Attempts** column on the TKNDrill Record, page 36.

For Job 3, place a dot where the vertical and horizontal lines intersect for the Job Number and EAM. (For the sample line it is at Job 3, 1.67 EAM.)

For Job 4 through Job 10, follow the procedure for Job 3 above. (For the sample line the intersection is at Job 4, 2.00 EAM.) Connect the dots with a line from the previous job to the present job. Progress in reducing Errors a Minute will be shown by a downward sloping line.

TECHNIQUE CHECKLIST, TEN-KEY TOUCH METHOD

Operator _____   Evaluator _____

Write the date in the proper space and place a check mark (✓) after a technique that is performed satisfactorily. Place a zero (0) after a technique that needs improvement.

Technique	Job								
	Date	3	4	5	6	7	8	9	10
Getting Ready									
1. Clears the desk of everything except materials needed for operating the calculator.									
2. Places the calculator in a position that allows the wrist and hand to be parallel to the keypad and allows the greatest freedom of finger movement over the keypad.									
3. Positions the book and the calculator at a comfortable angle so numbers can be read and written easily.									
4. Sits in a comfortable, erect position with feet flat on the floor for proper balance and minimum fatigue.									
5. Holds the operating arm with the wrist straight.									
6. Curves the fingers of the operating hand.									
7. Determines proper settings for decimals.									
8. Clears the register before starting a problem.									
Entering Numbers									
1. Strikes keys with a firm, quick stroke.									
2. Uses a rhythmic, bouncy touch.									
3. Depresses each key fully.									
4. Does not pause between strokes.									
5. Keeps eyes on the book and uses the touch method. Does not look at the keypad of the calculator.									
Proving and Verifying Answers									
1. Writes the answer legibly in the proper place.									
2. Checks the tape against the original problem.									
3. Proofreads the tape in the prescribed manner.									
4. Proves the answers in the prescribed manner.									
Attitude									
1. Enthusiastic about learning.									
2. Optimistic about improving.									
3. Confident about success.									
4. Alert but relaxed.									

CORRECTING ERRORS

An error can occur at the following different places in the calculating process.

1. **Before** a number is recorded on the tape

   If an error is detected before an operational key (any key other than a number key, including the +, −, ×, and ÷) is struck, do the following:

   a. Strike the Clear Key [3] to clear the incorrect number from the display window. Your calculator may have a Clear Right Digit Key [4] in addition to a Clear Key. Strike the Clear Right Digit Key to clear an incorrect digit at the right of a number. For example, if you strike *457* rather than *456*, the Clear Right Digit Key will clear the 7 rather than the entire number from the display window.

   b. Enter the correct number.

2. **After** a number has been recorded on the tape

   a. **Before** a total has been taken

   If an error is detected after an operational key has been struck, but before a total has been taken, do the following:

(1) Subtract (if the incorrect number was added) or add (if the incorrect number was subtracted) the incorrect number to cancel the error. (Review the illustrations.)

(2) Enter the correct number.

Correcting Addition Errors

Problem	Tape
	0. CA
731	
552	731. +
313	552. +
739	Incorrect Number→ 331. +
2,335	Correction (Subtract)→ 331. −
	313. +
	739. +
	2,335. *

Correcting Subtracting Errors

Problem	Tape
	0. CA
767	
−347	767. +
694	Incorrect Number→ 357. −
−423	Correction (Add)→ 357. +
691	347. −
	694. +
	423. −
	691. *

b. *After* a total has been taken

If an error is detected after an operational key has been struck and after a total has been taken, do the following:

(1) Tear your tape from the calculator and place it beside the problem. Proofread by comparing the number on the tape with the numbers in the problem. Find the omitted, extra, or incorrect number(s).

(2) Write the amount of the error and how to correct it to the right of the incorrect number on the tape. Add or subtract the amount of the error from the total and enter the correct number. (See the illustrations for correcting errors on the tapes.)

Correcting Addition Errors on the Tape

Problem		Tape
731		0. CA
552		
313		731. +
739		552. +
2,335	Incorrect Number→	3Ø3. +ₓ10
		739. +
		2,325. *
	Correction→	+ 10
	Correct Answer→	2,335

Problem		Tape
914		0. CA
316		
858		914. +
375	Incorrect Number→	3Ø1. +₊45
2,463		858. +
		375. +
		2,508. *
	Correction→	− 45
	Correct Answer→	2,463

Correcting Subtraction Errors on the Tape

Problem	Tape	Problem	Tape
767 −347 694 −423 691	0. CA 767. + Incorrect Number→ 357. −₊10 694. + 423. − 681. * Correction→ + 10 Correct Answer→ 691	389 −151 644 −281 601	0. CA 389. + 151. − 644. + Incorrect Number→ 271. −₋10 611. * Correction→ − 10 Correct Answer→ 601

Correcting Omitted and Extra Numbers on the Tape

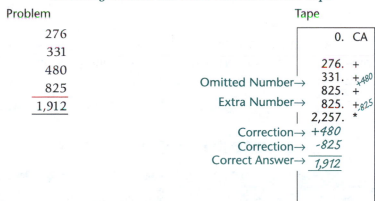

Problem	Tape
276 331 480 825 1,912	0. CA 276. + Omitted Number→ 331. +₊480 825. + Extra Number→ 825. +₋825 2,257. * Correction→ +480 Correction→ −825 Correct Answer→ 1,912

TECHNIQUE DRILLS A THROUGH F

Learning Objective

As you work each Technique Drill, concentrate so you can develop smooth, rhythmic touch techniques. Do not correct errors. Work each problem once. If you have time, repeat the drills.

Drill A

Tap the Addition Key without breaking your rhythm for entering numbers.

Drill B

Visualize the keypad and concentrate on the location of each key as you strike it. Keep your eyes on your book.

Drill C

Tap each key with a bouncy, rhythmic stroke.

Drill D

Concentrate on moving your fingers vertically from one key to the next. Curl your fingers to minimize arm movement.

Drill E

Try to maintain your rhythm throughout the problem as you move from one addend to the next. Your goal is to maintain your stamina (and breath) until the last addend is entered. Problems with fewer addends should now seem easier to complete.

Drill F

Keep your eyes on the digits in the problem. Try to maintain your stamina until the last addend is entered. Problems with fewer addends should now seem easier to complete.

Technique Drills

(A)	(B)	(C)	(D)	(E)	(F)
1	111	123	369	123	1,538
2	222	456	852	456	59,614
3	333	789	104	789	623,737
4	444	100	782	456	265
5	555	123	236	123	152,842
6	666	456	985	789	21,936
7	777	789	200	456	17,215
8	888	100	104	789	3,149
9	999	2,936	3,632	123	687,997
0	100			456	6,672
45	5,095			123	52,193
				789	122,852
				123	389
				456	17,463
				789	53,419
				456	684,736
				789	9,867
				456	39,138
				123	6,457
				789	23,172
				456	56,726
				789	108,951
				123	10,634
				456	165,914
				789	243,665
				12,066	3,170,541

Keep your fingers curved over the home-row keys.

APPENDIX G ·

SPEED DRILLS A THROUGH E

Learning Objective

As you work each Speed Drill, concentrate only on speed; ignore errors. If you have time, repeat the drills.

Drill A

Work the problem as many times as possible in one minute. Determine your SAM by counting one stroke for each digit, Addition Key, and Total Key on the tape. Record your SAM on the Speed Drill Record, page 48, beside the appropriate job number.

Drill B

Work the problem as many times as possible in one minute. Determine your SAM. Record your SAM on the Speed Drill Record, page 48.

Drill C

This problem has connectors, which means that the last digit in an addend (1,45<u>6</u>) is the first digit in the next addend (<u>6</u>83,774). Work the problem as many times as possible in one minute. Record your SAM.

Drill D

This problem does not have connectors. Work the problem as many times as possible in one minute. Determine your SAM. Record your SAM.

Drill E

Concentrate on maintaining speed with stamina. Work the problem as many times as possible in *three minutes*. Divide total strokes by three minutes to calculate your SAM. Record your SAM.

APPENDIX G

Speed Drills

	(A)		(B)		(C)		(D)		(E)
	111		123		1,456		4,135		1,538
	222		456		683,774		368,472		59,614
	333		789		45,046		46,504		623,737
	444		100	25 →	621,547	25 →	265,170		5,265
20 →	555	20 →	123		7,253		9,531	30 →	152,842
	666		456		331,014		730,143		21,936
	777		789		49,489		84,260		17,215
	888		100		90,265		10,652		23,149
	999		123	50 →	1,829,844	50 →	1,518,867		687,997
	000		45					30 →	6,672
40 →	4,995	40 →	3,104						52,193
									122,852
									4,389
									17,463
								30 →	53,419
									684,736
									59,867
									39,138
									6,457
								30 →	23,172
									6,726
									108,951
									1,063
									165,914
									4,366
								150 →	2,950,671

SPEED DRILL RECORD

Name _____

SAM for Speed Drills A through E

Instructions: Record SAM for the Skill Builder in each job.

Job	Date	A	B	C	D	E
SAMPLE	9/6	110	115	108	106	98
4						
5						
6						
7						
8						
9						
10						

ACCURACY DRILLS A THROUGH E

Learning Objective

As you work each Accuracy Drill, concentrate only on accuracy; ignore speed. If you have time, repeat the drills.

Drill A

Your speed should be reduced because no key is adjacent to the next key in each addend. Work the problem until you complete it without an error.

Drill B

This problem contains digits within addends that have similar configurations. For example, rounded digits (3, 6, 0, 9) and straight digits (1, 4, 7). Your speed should be reduced because you must distinguish between similar digits. Work the problem until you complete it without an error.

Drill C

This problem contains handwritten digits. Because they are somewhat difficult to read, you will need to reduce your speed. Work the problem until you complete it without an error.

Drill D

Concentrate on accuracy with stamina. Keep your eyes on the digits in the problem. Work the problem until you complete it without an error.

Drill E

Each of these five problems has the same answer, 77,777.

1. Work Problem 1.

   a. If your answer is correct, continue to Step 2.

   b. If your answer is not correct, repeat Problem 1 until you calculate the correct answer.

2. Work Problems 1 through 5 following the procedure in Step 1 until all problems are correct in the same attempt. For example, if you make an error in Problem 4, start again with Problem 1.

Accuracy Drills

(A)	(B)	(C)	(D)	(E) 1.	2.	3.	4.	5.
71,629	3,609	29,531	1,538	6,641	17,231	31,998	25,961	6,732
3,427	33,960	838,763	59,614	34,129	834	3,087	4,722	2,985
138,160	4,141	4,120	623,737	2,780	1,937	12,356	11,490	14,037
50,834	71,441	265,468	265	582	6,848	9,973	9,584	562
372,617	225	91,722	152,842	11,946	523	463	147	10,983
40,371	2,552	353,061	21,936	1,308	45,712	10,857	855	8,221
2,768	339	4,895	17,215	13,552	3,687	1,684	17,278	4,215
505,194	69,669	28,361	3,149	6,839	1,005	7,359	7,740	30,042
1,185,000	185,936	1,615,921	687,997	77,777	77,777	77,777	77,777	77,777
			6,672					
			52,193					
			122,852					
			389					
			17,463					
			53,419					
			684,736					
			9,867					
			39,138					
			6,457					
			23,172					
			56,726					
			108,951					
			10,634					
			165,914					
			243,665					
			3,170,541					

TEN-KEY NUMERIC DRILL #2

Margin labels (left, top to bottom): 50 strokes → · 25 strokes → · 50 strokes → · 25 strokes → · 50 strokes → · 25 strokes →

Top block

(A)	(B)	(C)	(D)	(E)
5,181	645,916	216,523	38,628	502,389
312,509	6,302	98,451	5,748	35,715
82,573	87,409	342,168		2,830
360,906	211,975	469,197		876,841
889,356	185,284	5,652		57,406
753,542	75,422	82,571		81,657
641	869,514	7,419		7,430
82,824	4,087	51,837		589,918
	53,277	16,323		
	4,975	758,927		
2,487,532	**1,928,099**	**1,373,885**	**1,690,247**	**2,154,186**

Middle block

(F)	(G)	(H)	(I)	(J)
325,389	235,604	52,983	5,798	33,241
509,738	96,364	156,751	971,486	931,229
7,654	84,722	720,598	31,264	57,692
14,816	47,712	3,107	447,428	60,946
730,259	129,569	8,539	95,387	57,252
186,872	7,845	145,249	15,245	492,963
43,497	96,214	78,984	193,531	82,742
562	48,242	15,643	6,461	2,976
1,818,787	**746,272**	**1,181,854**	**1,766,600**	**1,719,041**

Bottom block

(K)	(L)	(M)	(N)	(O)
82,081	529,174	26,378	718,295	903,681
134,509	2,036	268,829	2,165	77,193
3,422	65,124	4,875	367,921	1,664
349,605	181,787	749,321	84,946	205,068
9,166	54,519	135,182	751,322	4,620
74,189	407,841	6,285	16,862	713,598
205,923	8,535	44,617	1,044	339,976
73,596	78,145	70,325	46,909	7,596
932,491	**1,327,161**	**1,305,812**	**1,989,464**	**2,253,396**

TEST RECORD

Name _____

Complete this TEST RECORD following the instructions for the TKNDrill Record on page 37.

Test After	Date	Attempt	Total Strokes	Actual SAM	Total Errors	Actual EAM	Best of 3 Attempts SAM	EAM	Goal SAM	EAM	Grades (1) SAM	(1) EAM	(2) Total	(3) Avg
Sample	10/19	1	200	67	4	1.33			80	.33				
		2	216	72	2	.67								
		3	243	81	1	.33	81	.33			70	90	160	80
5 Hours (Job 5)		1												
		2												
		3												
10 Hours (Job 10)		1												
		2												
		3												

(1) Your instructor will provide information for these grades.

(2) Add grades for SAM and EAM.

(3) Divide Total by 2.

ANSWER STRIPS

JOB 4

Name _____

Date _____

1.	25
2.	599
3.	172
4.	3,181
5.	642
6.	474
7.	4,514
8.	1,382
9.	3,819
10.	27,636

JOB 2

Name _____

Date _____

1.	3,210
2.	3,199
3.	1,383
4.	3,418
5.	3,247
6.	1,525
7.	2,230
8.	646
9.	2,517
10.	1,596
11.	1,944
12.	2,416
13.	1,626
14.	2,518
15.	1,944
16.	1,893
17.	1,982
18.	5,745

JOB 1

Name _____

Date _____

1.	30
2.	180
3.	330
4.	321
5.	340
6.	328
7.	311
8.	330
9.	340
10.	319
11.	3,352
12.	3,251
13.	3,350
14.	3,226
15.	3,110

19. _____2,127_____
20. _____2,895_____
21. _____1,829_____
22. _____20,718_____
23. _____27,717_____
24. _____18,301_____
25. _____7,889_____
26. _____6,381_____
27. _____3,677_____
28. _____3,791_____
29. _____1,677_____
30. _____3,996_____
31. _____3,996_____
32. _____16,946_____
33. _____27,212_____
34. _____3,131_____
35. _____2,005_____
36. _____3,289_____
37. _____1,991_____
38. _____139,992_____
39. _____38,509_____
40. _____853,715_____
41. _____941,357_____

JOB 7

Name _____

Date _____

1. _____13_____
2. _____25_____
3. _____102_____
4. _____6_____
5. _____32_____
6. _____208_____
7. _____635_____
8. _____103_____
9. _____58_____
10. _____2_____

JOB 6

Name _____

Date _____

1. _____20_____
2. _____76_____
3. _____630_____
4. _____28,404_____
5. _____142,569_____
6. _____527,162_____
7. _____4,320,036_____
8. _____16,938,792_____

JOB 5

Name _____

Date _____

1. _____835,633_____
2. _____934,054_____
3. _____114,282_____
4. _____41,079_____
5. _____47,410_____
6. _____2,424_____
7. _____673_____
8. _____2,544_____
9. _____1,786_____
10. _____769_____
11. _____1,144_____
12. _____165_____
13. _____2,089_____
14. _____1,389_____
15. _____5,105_____

JOB 10

Name _____

Date _____

1. _____ 108 _____
2. _____ 2,832 _____
3. _____ 63,888 _____
4. _____ 185,196 _____
5. _____ 324,276 _____
6. _____ 9 _____
7. _____ 1 _____
8. _____ 27 _____
9. _____ 4 _____
10. _____ 46 _____
11. _____ 4,871 _____
12. _____ 4,810 _____
13. _____ 2,382 _____
14. _____ 12,063 _____
15. _____ 3,391 _____
16. _____ 665 _____
17. _____ 684 _____
18. _____ 2,717 _____
19. _____ 693 _____
20. _____ 18,881,114 _____

JOB 9

Name _____

Date _____

1. _____ 3,310 _____
2. _____ 3,530 _____
3. _____ 1,861 _____
4. _____ 1,845 _____
5. _____ 4,083 _____
6. _____ 4,065 _____
7. _____ 2,244 _____
8. _____ 2,202 _____
9. _____ 2,729 _____
10. _____ 2,771 _____
11. _____ 3,243 _____
12. _____ 3,181 _____

JOB 8

Name _____

Date _____

1. _____ 22,528 _____
2. _____ 10,766 _____
3. _____ 10,179 _____
4. _____ 43,473 _____
5. _____ 14,632 _____
6. _____ 7,184 _____
7. _____ 7,848 _____
8. _____ 29,664 _____
9. _____ 85,537 _____
10. _____ 20,467 _____
11. _____ 25,632 _____
12. _____ 39,438 _____
13. _____ 3,865 _____
14. _____ 2,764 _____
15. _____ 2,080 _____
16. _____ 3,181 _____
17. _____ 200 _____
18. _____ 99 _____
19. _____ 48 _____
20. _____ 84 _____

21. 57,936
22. 15,099,210
23. 34,038,260
24. 54
25. 141
26. 43
27. 238

21. 431
22. 44,060
23. 142,020
24. 126,990
25. 66,740
26. 379,810
27. 20
28. 39
29. 86
30. 24
31. 181
32. 616
33. 1,762
34. 232
35. 418
36. 3,028